GETTING FROM HERE TO THERE: RECLAIMING A LOST GENERATION

Keith E. Lindsey, Ph.D.

Foreword by Ebony Bowers, Ph.D.

GETTING FROM HERE TO THERE: RECLAIMING A LOST GENERATION

To those who believe change can happen...Think big!

OTHER PUBLICATIONS

The Economics of Health
The 12 Experiences

ABOUT THE AUTHOR

Dr. Keith Lindsey, a native of New York City, currently lives in Knoxville, Tennessee. He is a financial manager, adjunct professor, and consultant. He is the owner of the Lindsey Group, a multi-faceted consulting and referral business that focuses on health, educational, community, and financial concerns.

Keith earned his Bachelor of Science in Biology from Oakwood University, his Master of Public Health from East Tennessee State University, and his Doctorate of Philosophy in Public Health from Walden University.

He is the author of *The Twelve Experiences: Living with God, Living by Faith* and *The Economics of Health*. Keith does consulting with people and community groups to foster positive social change.

In his spare time, Keith enjoys reading, DIY projects, music, golf, martial arts, watching movies and sports, bike riding, and doing things with his wife, son, and dog.

Keith can be reached by e-mail at Thelindseygroup2@gmail.com.

ACKNOWLEDGEMENTS

I wanted to thank my sister, Kishia, for our hours of debating and arguing issues that provided me with insight and enlightenment to write this book.

I want to thank my wife, Charlene, for being my editor and reviewer.

To my good friend CC for always inspiring me to be a socially conscious thinker.

A special thanks to my friends, Dr. Ebony Bowers and Dr. Ellen Chism, for being great motivators.

CONTENTS

FOREWORD

Dr. Keith Lindsey and I met through a mutual friend because we needed some guidance to get through our dissertation process. Despite the guidance I received from my dissertation committee, Keith assisted me with making my dissertation process make sense to me in addition to making sure that the content would meet the academic standards of Walden University. Little did I know, what started as Keith being my dissertation guru, turned into him becoming a friend, a big brother, and an ally for enlightening about the modern black social consciousness.

As a black, educated, church going, divorced, single mother living in the South working to advance our community through nonprofit work within my community, this book hits home like no other. In my over three decades of life, I have seen the decline of black church leadership for social advances and turn into what Keith refers to as a "social club." This modern day social club needs to refocus itself on Biblical teachings, working inclusively within our communities to achieve social advocacy (for education, black on black crime, increase black incarceration, etc.), and try to avoid the "crabs in a bucket" mentality of keeping those that are trying to advance down.

Let's start working together and fight the need to do what society expects us to be, to be uneducated and to kill each other.

-Ebony Bowers, Ph.D., HS-BCP

PREFACE

Everyone who passes through this life realizes they are here for a finite period of time in which they hope to leave their mark on the world. Each generation throughout history has faced a trial that has defined their consciousness and developed a legacy that could be passed down to subsequent generations. Today, we are faced with the development of a generation who may not have a story to pass down. We are at the cusp of creating a "lost generation" that will certainly comprise a population headed down a road to nowhere.

The blame for this occurring does not lie with one particular event because this has been festering for years and is now beginning to rear its ugly head. This generation has been birthed

into a world blended with technology and media.
It is amazing to think how the events that has
occurred over the past 15-20 years have been so
effective in creating the perfect storm of
transforming a population into a socially driven
society!

I look at the picture of today's America and
the brightness of our future. I often think about
the mistakes we have made and the ability to
solve them. We are now facing a generation of
hate, mistrust, and oppression not seen since the
days of the Civil Rights Movement, except this
battle is now being captured on cellphones and
broadcast via social media.

Our internal struggle will prove to be our
undoing unless we make a conscious decision to
rise from the ashes of institutional slavery. Yes,

this form of slavery rose from entitlements, not valuing education, and having ineffective communities. However, we cannot simply say the problem is "black on black"; neither can we proclaim "the days of seeing race is over"; nor can we exclaim "it wasn't my family who did this to you" because these are excuses being uttered to avoid facing the issue and having a truthful discussion about race relations in the United States.

We cannot move forward until we collectively acknowledge there is a problem. We cannot move forward in the shadow of ignorance; we cannot move forward in the spirit of anger and hostility; we cannot move forward blaming each other for society's woes. We can move forward to realize the dream of Dr. King where people are no longer judged by their outward appearance, but are welcomed because of their spirit, character, and convictions.

However, society confuses success with progress because they misconstrue the principles of liberty, justice, and freedom. They misapply the notion of "becoming" and "arriving" in regards to being accepted in this country. In short, we cannot have true progress that builds towards unity because we refuse to acknowledge the systemic problems that plague our nation and prohibits true reconciliation.

One day we will be able to sit at the table of equality and have a real discussion about our problems. One day we will be able to gather together, break bread, and truly care about every citizen of this great nation. One day we will be able to stand side and side, hold hands, and truly say we are in this fight together for the betterment of all people. One day we will stop hyphenating our names and come to the realization we are all Americans. One day we will not have to ask each other what do we have to lose, but what can we collectively achieve. I believe this achievement will take people who are not afraid to call out problems and possess the fortitude to forge solutions.

I chose to write this book in order to discuss issues specifically facing Black America and how does our consciousness need to have a drastically different focus if we desire to see this generation of children prosper. In fact, we are harming them by not being parents, disciplinarians, and good custodians. We are losing this generation to music, sports, and other forms of disruptive entertainment. College is not for them because they are comfortable with making "easy money" instead of putting in the sweat equity needed to make an honest dollar. They embrace the criminal element instead desiring to be a law abiding citizen.

This will truly be a lost generation unless we stop letting others dictate our path and direction. The journey starts now...

COMMUNICATION

When it comes to communication, I am not going to write this chapter in 144 characters or less, even though this is the present way most people communicate. Communication is what separates making the deal from thinking about the deal. In short, the ability to communication will be one of the pitfalls of this generation as we wonder why we cannot be better power players in society.

Now we have cut on the television and watched the media interview a black person and wonder aloud about how they manage to select the one person who makes your skin crawl as soon as they begin to speak. This is not to be cruel or insensitive, but it is fundamentally important that a person, regardless of race/creed/nationality, should be able to put together a coherent statement. Some of the greatest black leaders were very efficient orators; Dr. King, Malcolm X, Frederick Douglass, Thurgood Marshall, and Andrew Young to name a few. They were powerful in deeds, but their words delivered a power that transformed the consciousness of people at a time when it was sorely needed for change.

Malcolm X was a gifted orator and trained his best student Louis Farrakhan. They spoke among similar lines for blacks to develop their community, transcend the division of human life, and walk a different path towards personal enlightenment.[1] Even today, we have a host of black orators who can deliver messages of hope and faith to the masses. However, Black

America is plagued with the "I must be the most important person" syndrome, which is why thoughtful communication often falls by the wayside. Black America is afflicted by a lack of trust, a lack of empathy, a lack of sympathy, and the refusal to call a spade a spade. We live in a world of political correctness, but sometimes there is a need to be politically incorrect, to have the gloves come off, and speak with authority.

There are people out here who believe blacks cannot achieve because we cannot understand the English language. There are people out here who believe blacks should take ESL courses because the English language is a foreign language to blacks. There are people out here who believe blacks will never possess the communicative skills required to actively reason, discern, or disseminate information.

This is the reality of the 21st century as blacks strive to change opinions and stereotypes; however, this change must first be internalized prior to its acceptance by the community at large. Legrand Clegg featured an article that stated blacks do not speak English, they speak ebonics and this is what should be taught to their children in order for them to learn.[2]

This thought was reinforced by a college professor who stated the reason for high drop-out rates in the black community is directly correlated to being limited English speakers.[3] Moreover, he stated black children have to understand knowledge that is not being presented in their own language, and making

4

ebonics the official language of black people could help them master the English language.[4] So blacks who live in America do not speak English? This is a part of the communication breakdown and ignorance if people believe blacks cannot master the primary language of this society.

We do have communication problems, but this stems from idolizing popular culture and internalizing the need to not sound "white" as a part of black culture. Blacks have ascribed to this thinking so much that it has become the norm in black society. It has become a part of the black culture to think bad grammar is acceptable grammar.

Blacks have been conditioned to accept using slang as common language and view the use of proper English as selling out. We have been conditioned to accept this false language (ebonics) as a cultural identity instead of calling it what it really is, a way to keep us ignorant and untouchable.

I remember taking a fundamental of public speaking class in college where the professor taught us how to deliver different types of speeches. As a result, I learned it is not about the substance or depth of information one might have, it is important to be able to share this information with a wide variety of people with different backgrounds and experiences. It is similar to completing a dissertation where everyone might not fully understand the research, but should be able to comprehend the topic and points that are being made in the document.

So yes, I will be the first to admit people have different language styles. I will also surmise this is directly attributed to cultural differences. I will also admit most of it is a learned behavior and is changeable. I will admit black words are purposefully spoken in a way to not only sound ignorant, but to portray a false sense of self-worth, importance, and position.

Communication is one of the pillars of humanity. Blacks must be willing to not accept ebonics as their way of communicating because this only serves to divide and create an even deeper racial gulf. Our inability to master the language in their eyes makes us appear to be overly hostile in our communication, always speaking in angry overtures, and disengages us from important discussions.

When we are able to effectively communicate and dialogue, take notice how conversations will change or even cease because they know we can be self-thinkers. When your communication skills are weak, it is much harder to stand on issues and talk about them because of the inability to express thoughts. This leads to using foul language, louder tones, and aggressive speech in an attempt to express an opinion.

We can do better; we have to do better because our future is at stake. We have to understand our ability to communicate builds bridges, tears down walls, and can move people to improve relationships. However poor communication could build walls, shatter confidence, and destroy relationships.

America believes blacks cannot exist in a normal society because of what we represent. We have to create new narratives and tell new stories to celebrate the positive contributions of blacks in this country. We have to stand up and tell our story in a way similar to other races and nationalities have spoken about their plights and concerns.

This story is getting more unfamiliar with each passing generation because of the increased use of technology and lack of communication with our elders. We have gone from a call me tonight generation to we can "talk" through chatting and other forms of social media. This use of "non-traditional" communication

9

illustrates the change placed in the value of communication. Renita Schiavo stated that socializations, traditions, and values are important in determining how people perceive and receive communication and what outcomes may arrive from it.[5]

How do we improve our communication to effect change? We must first be willing to recognize the changing of the times and the cultural significance of the change. We must be willing to possess the patience required to reestablish a lost connection that was years in the making.

We must be willing to acknowledge this change will take time, sweat, and energy. We must also be willing to accept we might not be able to be put the genie of dysfunction back into the bottle. No matter what course of action is taken, we must be able to realize that time is not necessarily on our side, and we must be proactive in our efforts if change is the outcome we seek.

This is important because Black America cannot effectively fight for change if we cannot communicate this change to the world. We cannot obtain positive networks if we cannot express our views, goals, and plans. We cannot expect people to follow us in the struggle if we cannot explain to them the who, what, why, and how of the struggle in order to gain their confidence and support.

We cannot get to yes, if we cannot get past hello. We cannot make a statement if we do not have the voice to give the words life. We cannot be an effective leaders if we cannot communicate with confidence.

The art of communication is a very particular skill that cannot be performed in 144 character or less. It will take great resolve to overcome this barrier because it affects blacks in so many ways. Developing the art of communication will carry Black America a long way to get out in front of issues and turn silence in productive conversations.

THE BLACK FAMILY

The black family is a very interesting topic because it has dramatically changed from better to worse with each subsequent generation. It would be safe to say the breakdown of the black nuclear family has led to many of the problems we are facing in our schools and communities across the country. Most would not agree with this assessment and say the root of the problem lies in what has been done to blacks in America. However, this argument can be countered by simply revealing data and other statistics that will say otherwise.

As of 2014, there were 12 million black households in the United States.[6] As with any home, the power and responsibility of molding the minds of the next generation of leaders

13

resides with mothers and fathers acting in a co-parenting role. Mothers are the nurturers and fathers are the character builders.

They are not simple roles because they require sacrifice, vision, guidance, and active surveying to ensure their children are being instilled with the values and morals that will make them productive citizens. Dean Kalahar stated the psychology of children are stronger in two parent homes versus those who do not because they could suffer from esteem and self-discipline problems.[7]

The destruction of the black family in today's society is the continuation of the divide and conquer strategy practiced during slavery times. When the Africans were brought to this country they were isolated from their fellow tribesmen and families. They were stripped of their cultural identities and forced to submit their wills to their new slave masters. They were stripped of their integrity, self-esteem, and pride by being forced to carry "white names." They were kept illiterate by their slavemasters so they would not be able to understand the freedoms they truly possessed in the new land.

Is this really the reality in which we live? Is it possible to theorize that we are still succumbing to the same practice in the 21st century? Sadly, the answer is yes because we have not learned from our past to build a better future. Here are some alarming and disturbing statistics:[8]

➢ In 2009, 73% of black children were born to unmarried mothers.

➢ In the 1980s and 90s, an absolute majority of those black families with no husband present lived in poverty.

➢ 54% of all black children were living only with their mothers after 1965 until 1992.

This might be difficult to accept, but here are more statistics to highlight the decline of the black nuclear family:[9]

➢ 45% of black households are comprised of a married couple, compared to 80% for Whites, and 70% for Hispanics.

➢ In 1890, 80% of black households were comprised of two parents. One hundred years later, this number has fallen to 40%.

➢ Blacks are significantly less likely than other racial/ethnic groups to ever marry, be less likely to remarry, be more likely to divorce, separate or cohabitate, and bear and rear children out of wedlock.

➢ The low rate of marriage and high divorce rate in the black community are decreasing the black middle class.

➢ Blacks are simply not willing to commit to marriage and have stable families.

➢ Blacks are more happy to birth children out of wedlock and have "baby daddies and baby mommas" instead of building a strong nuclear family.

The miscarriage of justice for the black family is in the comfort of foregoing the traditional family structure to live a life where confusion is the normal. It is now a place where men and women fight over whose gender should be the most dominant in the household. Kay

Hymowitz stated the rise of feminism conditioned the struggling black woman to believe she was strong and did not need to rely on a traditional family status to survive.[10] She further went on to state the decline of the black family cripples communities and damages the psychological and social ability of children.[11]

The unraveling of the black family is not a figment of anyone's imagination because we have a majority of our children living in single parent homes. We are faced with lower economic opportunities; lower educational expectations, and are dying at an alarming rate. The nucleus of the black family is dying from within, yet we are crying out in protest because of the pressure being applied from the external conflicts affecting our community.

How can the black community succeed when they have children born into unstable homes, are poorly educated, and suffer from reduced economic power? How does a community thrive, survive, or rebound from this epidemic? Yes, the word epidemic is being used to describe this information point because like a disease, this problem poses a direct threat to the survival of the black family. If left unchecked, this growing phenomenon could lead to us losing future generations of leaders, community servants, advocates, and activists.

In addition, here are some other issues faced by children living in single parent homes:[12]

➢ Children living in father absent homes don't fare well economically.

> They experience higher poverty rates in comparison to other races (24%).

> They are approximately twice as likely to conceive children out of wedlock when they are teens or young adults.

> 70% of all young people in state reform institutions were raised in fatherless homes.

So the breakdown of the home is the beginning of a poor start in life for children of color. The stability produced by a solid nuclear family is being replaced by "strong black women" who feel they don't need family structure, imprisoned fathers/mothers, and having multiple children with multiple men/women. Since most black children are products of single mother homes, I am going to focus on the black male who should be in the father role.

The lack of a father in the home could lead to spiritual deficiencies and financial instability for the mothers who must assume the "be all-do all" role. David Blankenhorn referred to the lack of a father in a child's life as paternal disinvestment and describes how delineates the difference simple biological paternity and being a real father.[13] The lack of stability in a home could be directly transferred to the child because a father's lack of involvement could lead to the child having increased delinquency, foster behavioral and social integration issues, become involved with gangs, or exhibit other character issues.

Fatherhood goes beyond simply paying child support, as most would refer to as a "pay to play" system. This is the system where the father is refused contact unless he pays some form of child support, not realizing the greatest payment to the child is not the money the mother receives, but having a father who truly desires to be a part of their child's life. Our society, though misguided, is preaching to women that they do not need a man to be a father to their children. This was not always the culture of the black community; however, the advent of the women empowerment movement has shifted the minds and opinions about the nuclear family.

The traditional roles of the family have also changed. The father, whom I liken to a Fortune 500 CEO, cannot be in charge of a shell business. This shell represents the black man who is absent from the home. This causes the mother to be the CEO and the Chief Nurturing Officer (CNO).

The father in this picture was the disciplinary judge, provider, and head of the moral police. No wonder our children are so captivated by immoral activities! Now being a man is not how well respected he is or how much he is loved by his children, it is based on a total immoral concept. This concept is generated by society's hypersensitive view of the black man as an overaggressive, sports dominated figure, whose lack of worthwhile contributions to society make them worthy of extermination.

In the black community being a man does not equate to being educated, well versed, and well dressed; in fact, the opposite rings true.

Why? Because intellect is equated to being a traitor to their race and culture. The thoughts and actions of this generation leads to the vilification of the black male and their place in society. Blankenhorn stated the lack of good fathers leads to a devalued sense of manhood that is passed on to children.[14] Blankenship powerfully stated about the lack of fatherhood that "a decultured fatherhood thus produces a doubtful manhood."[15]

The home should be a safe haven for children. There is an increased chance for dysfunction in the home with the absence of a parent. What type of environment could one expect to exist when there is a rotating door of men and women; one where the atmosphere is tense with anger and intolerance; one where yelling is the norm?

Laurence Steinburg stated children benefit from being raised in a positive environment versus one that has an unstable foundation.[16] Children emulate what they see, so it is vital for children to see the home as a model for good behaviors.

The lack of fathers in a child's life does upend the balance of this equation. Today, good fathers are in demand because they are an endangered species. Yes, an endangered species because there are so few good black men who accept their role as a man, father, role model, and teacher.

With the vast number of black men behind prison walls, on drugs, illiterate, and uneducated makes the situation in the black community even harder to endure. In this age, we are losing our children because we are failing them in the home. We are failing to give them a good moral compass because we want to be their friends instead of being parents.

Good black men are indeed in an endangered classification in this day and age. The strong, traditional black family is being replaced by society's failed experiment on family. We no longer have kings and queens working together in the home for the betterment of the community; we have kings with multiple queens; queens with multiple kings; queens with queens; kings with kings; and queens doing it alone with the king staring from afar.

The time will come when we will have to decide what is more important for the sake of our families and communities. We will either have to stand up for what is right, or lay down to follow the whims of society's failed experiment. The destabilization of the black nuclear family has become one of the pillars of the existing problem; however, we have to rebuild the black family to change our way of thinking, which will in turn transform our opinions of self and how we treat each other.

RELIGION

Blacks and religion have shared a unique pairing since the days of the slavery. It was the religious experience of blacks that provided the courage and perseverance to endure the horrors of slavery. The singing of Negro Spirituals strengthened their spirits as they sung "Wade in the Water", "Swing Low, Sweet Chariot", "Steal Away", and "Go Down Moses."

In the days of slavery, Christianity was not the religion of the slave because slave owners believed the slave did not have a soul. The institution of slavery was justified through "Christian" principles; however, the religion used to justify slavery would soon became the clarion call for the slave's deliverance. The God of Christianity for whites could never be on par with blacks, and they feared an uprising would occur if the slaves learned the Christian principles of freedom, redemption, and equality.

The heightened role of singing and praying for deliverance was not any different from the Israelites crying out for freedom from Egyptian bondage. God remembered His promise and answered their call by sending Moses to deliver them. God did not turn His back on His people in the past and He has not done so in the present. However, are we still petitioning for deliverance or are we satisfied with the status quo? The response to this question will require an introspective view into the drastic changes in the black community.

The role of religion in the black community has been one that has been sorely disappointing with each subsequent generation. This change has been felt when only 20% of black people attend church, while another percentage claim to be spiritual, unaffiliated, or simply do not believe. This might be the genesis of understanding why the black community has had a severe disconnect with one another and how it has been instrumental in the breakdown of the community.

Once upon a time the black church was the bedrock of the community. People respected the church, came to the church for assistance, and looked to the church to be the leader in the community's civil and social issues. Ask someone from the 50s and 60s about the relationship between the church and movement and they will proclaim how the church was the foundation for spreading, encouraging, and nurturing the Civil Rights Moment.

Revs. Dr. King, Lowery, Jackson, Abernathy and other men of the cloth stood strong and steadfast in their belief that the Creator of the world did not create two separate societies for His children. Despite the push back from society at large, the church was a safe place for blacks to congregate and worship. The church was the place where the people received the spiritual strength and physical fortitude to overcome the politics, policies, and practices of the oppressive and segregated south.

In delving further into the establishment of black religion in America one would have to travel back to the days of slavery. Christianity, a religion of peace and service, was used to

31

validate the institution of slavery in this country. However, blacks were introduced to the revelation of worship that focused on inclusion, freedom, and tolerance in part by the work of Richard Allen, Hiram Revels, William Seymour, Thomas Dorsey, Howard Thurman, and Peter Williams.

The Pew Research Center stated 94% of blacks consider themselves to be protestant.[17] However, what is the link between this religious experience and the community? How does this translate into blacks engaged in church–related activities translate into community activism? It does not if they do not actively practice what they profess. Pew also presented the following statistics regarding blacks and their religious experience:[18]

- 75% of blacks stated religion was important to them, however 53% attend church either twice a year or not at all.
- 61% do not participate in study/education activities.
- 72% have no clear standard of right or wrong.
- 24% do not read the bible.
- 80% believe in heaven.
- 73% believe in hell.
- 14% do not pray on a regular basis.
- 57% do not look to religion for guidance about right or wrong

The data reveals why the black church does not possess the power for change in the community.

As a result, the black community no longer looks to the church for guidance and direction.

The moral compass, mentoring, spiritual coping skills that the church provides are not being taken advantage of by the community. Most will exclaim this is happening because the church is not keeping up with the times; the younger generation is not looking for a regimented service; and the church is not helping them grow spiritually.

This generation is searching for a service that will be one hour or less in duration, will not talk about how to better their lives, and does not want to hear that the life they are living is not acceptable. In other words, they want the comfort to feel accepted, but do not have the desire to be challenged to become a better person through a spiritual awakening. In this sense, possessing a lower spiritual aptitude could be a direct correlation to the growing unease in the community.

There was a time when members of a church lived in the neighborhood, helped look out for the neighborhood, and people had respect for the religious people on the block. The church was a second parent, sometimes a first, and served as a moral compass to individuals. It was a place for mentoring, for counseling, for guidance, for direction, for getting kids straight, and for spiritual growth.

The black church has lost this connection because the parishioners no longer live in the neighborhood. They still come in to worship in the neighborhood, but they do not have the same effect on the community. This is a direct impact of the black migration from the black neighborhoods because the more affluent areas of living that were denied to blacks became accessible.

The black community is now experiencing black flight where successful blacks no longer desire to work on building their community from within, they want to do it from afar and envision having the same effect. This is almost like a person looking down from a high perch wondering how life is for people down on the ground. They appear to be miniscule to the eye, but they have real life problems that might never be understood unless they are being met on their level.

What is the future of symbolic bond between the black church and the black community? Said Sewell stated black pastors were moving towards the mindset that the church might not be able to advance the needs of the black community.[19] This was the answer provided from a direct survey of pastors in a southern city, so another question might be asked to how this could relate to the mindset of black pastors in other urban and rural areas.

The black church, which once stood for inclusion, is on the cusp of being an exclusive club, where one is judged by their looks, job status, family status, and appearance. The issue of the black disconnect from religion could be one reason for the black church becoming disconnected from the community.

Dr. Joseph Washington stated the black church has gone from being a place of spiritual building to a socialization center, and that it no longer has the feeling of a place where all can be accepted.[20] Faith and family, the hallmark of the early church, has been replaced with logic and finances. Dr. Washington in his passage also discussed how the black church must find a way to combine theology with learning about the community and family.[21] There should not be a huge amount of confusion and disagreement on this point because in order to change a community one must get back to the foundation of the problem, the deterioration of the black nuclear family.

In our warped sense of reality, the church has no longer become a hospital for the sick, it has become a money making venture. It is not overly concerned about outreach, it is more concerned with looking important to city officials and blacks of "importance." The church is losing its own spiritual and moral compass, so its effectiveness for outreach is like providing antibiotics for a virus, it will not have an effect.

The black church rose from the ashes of slavery. It rose from the beatings, raping, and killing of blacks inflicted upon them from their oppressors. The Negro Spiritual songs told the story of how blacks overcame the atrocities of slavery by embracing their deep rooted faith in God.

The songs brought out a message of deliverance by God, whom they believed would one day deliver them in a way similar to Him freeing the Israelites from the hand of the Egyptians. Those spirituals represented a feeling of spiritual freedom because their physical body was shackled. In turn, the masters could not break the backs of the slaves because they knew their redeemer.

Fast forward to the 21st century where the oppression still exists but under a different guise. The church has to deal with the enemy from within. It has to deal with the prosperity gospel; the get rich pastor; the lack of teaching from the bible; the clock checkers; the seat fillers; the unsupportive member; and the self-serving member.

The church is lacking male leadership to serve as positive role models for young boys. The church is in need of men and women who desire to be spiritual advocates to our dying communities. The community is in need spirit-filled people who are not afraid to face issues and be a pillar of support for those who need a voice.

During the civil right moment, the black church was a safe place for organizers to plan and strategize their moments. The church's role was similar to safe stations for the Underground Railroad, a pipeline for slaves to escape the oppression of the south to freedom in the north. Today, the church should be a safe zone for those who need spiritual guidance, moral correcting, and a mental boost. It is still the place for addressing issues that plague the black community and provide solutions or suggestions to tackle these issues.

On the role of the black church for this generation, Barbara Savage said, "Some thought of black Christianity as a "slave religion" that had run its course and lost its political and spiritual potency to meet the new demands of a more modem struggle against racial oppression."[22] How does the church remain a viable source of spiritual direction and morality? How does the church remain true to its calling while trying to expand its function in society at large? These questions and many more are on the thoughts and minds of ministers and parishioners across this great nation.

Despite the changes in society, the church should never compromise itself to "fit in" with society. Most ministers will soundly declare they follow the scriptures, yet they go quiet when certain subjects are mentioned because they do not wish to offend their base. In some ways, the church has morphed into mini-political units, not desiring to offend their largest supporters or alienate their congregations.

Marilyn Mellowes stated the black church, in regards to slavery, still defines blacks by philosophically connecting them to past events.[23] The conversation regarding religion and the community now becomes a discussion about how to bridge the moral gulf affecting the black community and whether the church is in a place to be an effective instrument of change.

The power of the church is in the people and the power to change communities rest in the church's ability to not sit back and let others take the lead. Most people feel that pastors only look to glorify and exalt themselves and will not lend their services to a program unless they can assume total control. At the same time, the people are willing to cede absolute control to pastors to the point where they cannot think for themselves, but will only act according to the word of the pastor. Therefore the pastor cannot serving in an advisory/teaching capacity, the pastor becomes the sole authority of determining whether a program or activity should be allowed. For most, this dictatorial style of authority could be the reason why many are turned off to organized religion.

The black church is in need of people who just don't claim to be religious, it is in desperate demand for people who are willing to roll up their sleeves and work inside and outside the church. The church is in a battle with a generations of blacks who are more concerned with money, power, and position than their spiritual lives. A generation more concerned with tasting the "American dream" and looking out for themselves instead of caring about what affects them and the community. They are preoccupied with immoral deeds and questionable actions and are more concerned with their physical appearance instead of building communities.

The black church, once a strong pillar of the community, has become a drive-thru because the people desire instantaneous results. The black community suffers because many of the successful and influential blacks move out of the neighborhood for greener pastures that also affects the church. The future generations of blacks do not understand the need for church because it is not modeled or incorporated into the family.

The revitalization of the black church does not start with attracting members, it begins with the church returning to its roots of teaching, advocacy, and service. The black church needs to remember its past, be an advocate in the present, and be willing to change the future by embracing positive change. This is and always has been the mission of the church, now the church has to reposition itself to remain faithful to this charge.

There is still a need for the church in our society despite being buffeted by the winds of uncertainty and apathy. The church must remain a beacon to the community. The freedom train's bell is ringing loud throughout the black community, we must be willing to educate the

community and get them on board.

EXPECTATIONS

The word expect can be a powerful and motivating word. Our parents told us as children what they expected from us in regards to our behavior and manners. As students, we are provided with classroom expectations from our teachers and instructors in the form of a syllabus. On our jobs we are given expectations in the form of a job description. In short, our whole lives are built and shaped by various levels of expectations. The question that most ask and few answer is how we handle these expectations in the face of those who think so little of us.

From the birth of this country, blacks were considered property, and were treated worse than animals. Stripped of their culture, language, and ethnicity; they were forced to acclimate to the will and whim of their slave masters. The expectations of blacks then is not very different of the expectations held today. Society expects us to be killers, rappers, thugs, deadbeats, and athletes. However, this grave mischaracterization of blacks has gone on for so long that many believe this narrative to be true, a behavior known to sociologists as the looking glass self.

The looking glass self is a self-reflection of how a person or group is perceived by others. Charles Cooley stated a person's growth and development is based on a combination of society's interactions and perceptions.[24] The perception of blacks in this country is we should be happy for what we have received, do not complain, and go on with your life. There is no room for protesting, peacefully or otherwise, because you do not have the right. In other words, you do not have to be worried about social justice issues; you do not have to be concerned about economic issues; you do not have to be concerned with the political justice system; and you do not have to worry about the educational system because someone else will tend to it on your behalf.

The power of expectation is connected to the power of perspective. Blacks face a daily challenge in regards to the overbearing power of perception that molds our expectations. If you tell your child they will never amount to anything, 9 times out of 10 they will become what you expected them to be in life. The frame of the Black experience is changing because the past expectations and present recognitions are evolving.

When Barack Obama was elected President of the United States (POTUS), many blacks had an unrealistic expectation that his ascent to the greatest office in the land would mean all of Black America would also automatically ascend. The unrealistic expectation of pushing the "black agenda" would years later find him being called on the carpet for not living up to their vote's expectations. The change that was hoped and desired for did not occur as they dreamed, so now President Obama was seen as a failure in the eyes of the Black America. However, they forget President Obama's role as POTUS placed him not as the leader of Black America, but president of all the citizens of the country.

Today, we are still faced with prejudiced expectations about black achievement and advocacy. Blacks can be athletes, but do not dare be an advocate for an issue because you are paid to play sports, not to be a visible voice to any problems. In other words, we are paying for your silence so know your place in this system, know what role you are supposed to play and shut your mouth. Anthony Robbins and Joseph McClendon stated "injustice and prejudice are the cancers of our society, and we must fight them tooth and nail every step of the way."[25] However, some of our external problems are blinded by our internal ones.

We have great expectations to be thinkers, movers, and educators; yet we treat each other like we are the enemy. Blacks are indeed hated by their own for their success, so the expectation to want and do more is frowned upon and is not considered as "being black." For example, we do not like people who are smart and articulate; our women do not find educated, polished men attractive; our men do not find women who have a sense of pride about them appealing; and we all can agree we do not like people who can put a sentence together. We lower our own expectations of each other by wanting our children to be the next Michael, Kobe or LeBron; we cheapen their expectations by thinking the only way to escape our situation is through sports; and we dilute our educational power by settling for certificates of attendance, which is when you spend four years in high school but do not graduate with a diploma.

We are expected to complain about the government, yet we relish from its benefits that has created a welfare state. We are expected to be gunned down by those sworn to serve and protect us. We are expected to blame ourselves for the atrocities that occur.

Thomas Sewell wrote an op-ed piece in the Knoxville News Sentinel that stated favors by politicians have hurt blacks, mentioned how educational standards and welfare have set blacks backwards, and called the favors a "declaration of moral bankruptcy."[26] It might be safe to say he might have forgotten the years of programming that must now be unplugged due to the harsh and racist conditions of slavery and Jim Crow.

Certain segments of the population believe that blacks are supposed to accept being mistreated in this country. We are supposed to ignore our history and watch people denigrate us for mentioning the horrors of slavery, but in response we have been told to bury the past. We are expected to forget the mistakes of the past or simply "go back" to where you came from. We are expected to be happy about our life's situation, and simply keep quiet as if it is an outdated issue. We are expected to think our lives do not matter, but we equally do not have the right to question others groups who gripe about their ordeals.

We are trapped in a cycle of expectation versus perceived reality. We are being lead to believe we do not possess the ability to think for ourselves. We are being taught the only way to escape our generational poverty is through investing in charter schools where certain children can attend. We are not expected to attend or even graduate from college, and if we do attend the professors do not think we possess the academic strength to be there in the first place. We are intimidated to not speak out about issues due to the fear of job demotion, retaliation, or termination.

Once again we revolve to the word expect, but now with a different twist. What do we expect from one another? How much do we push each other to strive for excellence through our own expectations? There is nothing wrong with having a goal to reach because it means the train of success will not be derailed. Sometimes there might be delays, but the train will keep running on the track.

Let's think about the Olympic torch as another example. The torch is designed to not be extinguished under ordinary circumstances and the organizers do everything in their power to ensure the flame does not go out. Even more, the cauldron that the torch lights is designed to remain ablaze for the entirety of the games.

For blacks, this torch represents freedom, power, tolerance, patience, deliverance, perseverance, and endurance. However, the torch needs to be protected from those who desire to snuff out its flame. Blacks carry the flame as light bearers to shine light into a society filled with prejudice, racism, and hate.

Expectations can be a two-edged sword because on one end it cuts deep, and other end is serrated to cause damage on the way out. However this damage is not physical in nature, but it is evolutional in regards to changing the way people think. The protesters and the other people fighting for the equal application of law fully comprehend the sense of lawlessness that is growing in our community. They perceive the problem will not get better nor will inaction lead to the achievement of a higher standard of living. The power of expectation for the black community must either lead to solutions, create a new generation of thinkers, or be faced with the reality of self-destruction.

POLITICS

Blacks and politics, a tradition that has been in the making since the founding of this country is one where blacks are still trying to grow and progress. Blacks have been used as political pawns on the electorate chessboard since the drafting of the United States Constitution. The laws and rights that were being trumpeted were not created with blacks in mind. In fact, since blacks in the early colonial days were slaves, a compromise was brokered to have them represented as three-fifths of a person. This was done in complete irony because the Constitution declared that all men are equal.

This percentage did not represent the slave, but the slave's economic and legislative value. So what kind of rights did the fractional slave possess? None would be the appropriate answer because the slaves were treated worse than animals. This fight would continue to our present society where blacks are still being labeled as economic factors to be considered by our elected officials.

During the harsh years of slavery, blacks and other minorities were used as cheap labor to build the infrastructure of this country. In return, blacks were denigrated, beaten, raped, pillaged, and treated to less than humane living conditions. Legally, blacks were subjected to illiteracy, poverty, and unable to voice their rights. Politically, this was supported by the local elected officials of the day, many of whom owned slaves and operated plantations of their own. It would be pure hyperbole to own slaves and then legislate against their own interest.

Blacks were just not fighting people for their freedom, they were contending against a system who used the laws of the land to jointly overpower and enslave them. Dr. Cornell West said about this struggle that slavery was "institution that leaves a very imprint on Black minds and Black bodies and constraints on Black political and economic power."[27] The struggle for freedom was strong during the early periods of this country's history; however, laws were passed to benefit, endorse, and protect the institution of slavery.

The slaves were not bound by the Constitution, but by a repressive and oppressive slave code. The initiation of these codes

produced other laws in the youthful years of the
United States:

➢ Congress allowed slavery importation for 20
years after ratifying the Constitution.

➢ Congress passed the Fugitive Slave Law that
allowed slave owners to retrieve their
"property" if they ran away.

➢ The Northwest Ordinance kept slavery alive
in the southern states, but not in the northern
states.

➢ The Missouri Compromise banned slavery
in states above the 36th line of latitude.

➢ The compromise of 1850 allowed new states
to decide if they wanted to be either a free or
slave state by popular vote.

➢ The Dred Scott decision announced by the
Supreme Court stated Dred Scott (slave) had

no political standing for freedom under the
Constitution, and could not sue for his
rights.

Blacks were still used as political pawns as the
first shots rang out in South Carolina signifying
the end of the perfect union.

The fight for blacks as an economic power
reached its climax in this war because the
southern states felt the government had no right
to tell them how to live their lives. However,
the northern states believed the slaves should be
free to migrate north. Again, this was a political
plan to ascertain which section of the country
controlled the congress through population
density numbers. Hence the real reason for the
Civil War was for economic and political power,
not for the freedom of the slaves.

Abraham Lincoln did not desire for the country to be engaged in war. His rationale for the war was not freedom, but to preserve the Union. He then had to use his political capital to create and issue the Emancipation Proclamation, which freed the slaves in the confederate states. After the war, the passages of the 13th, 14th, and 15th Amendments to the Constitution provided voting, freedom, and the abolishment of slavery. These amendments led to the creation of the Jim Crow Laws that would be enacted and enforced in the south until the passing of the Civil Rights Act. The southern states accomplished this by rewriting their constitutions, instituting poll taxes, and literacy test.[28]

The states enacted policies designed to prevent blacks from achieving goals; yet this was a flawed system maintained by those in power. The power of local politics played a crucial role in maintaining a separate but equal doctrine of the races in this country. Now it does not mean blacks have not held political offices or have been represented in political issues; however, blacks have never been considered equal in the creation or adjudication of laws. This push for equality led to the birth of the National Association for the Advancement of Color People (NAACP), who through its body fought inside and outside the courtroom for justice and equality.

In the days of Malcolm X and Dr. King there was a call for political and social justice, knowing the existing climate of the country could not be changed unless the laws were changed to level the playing field. However, this has not precluded blacks from having an opportunity to sit at the political table. This was very prevalent in the states of South Carolina and Louisiana during the post-reconstruction, where blacks were able to be elected to serve in the U.S. Congress. However, many whites did not like blacks assuming these positions and sought to reaffirm their authority through violence and intimidation.[29]

Today, blacks represent a large voting bloc in political landscape, yet only 59.6% are registered voters, and less than half voted in the 2012 presidential election.[30] The ability to court voters is one thing, exercising this political muscle is another contentious matter. This becomes increasingly difficult because 7.7% of blacks cannot vote due to legal constraints.[31] The election of President Barak Obama did not signify an end to race concerns in this country, it served as a beacon to magnify the issue and create an even more intolerable landscape.

Donald Trump summed up the landscape of blacks in the political spectrum when he boldly proclaimed "What the hell do you have to lose?" Most blacks would take this in an offensive tone; however, the question still looms without an appropriate response. What have the political parties done to earn our votes? What policies have been enacted to further the economic, educational, and social foundation of the black community? This is where the rubber must meet our proverbial road.

In this political world we are faced with having only partial justice served coupled with a perceived lack of empathy from any who do not agree with the message. Our political message is getting swallowed up by the continued fight for reparations and entitlements; however; we must not lose sight on what has been gained and our future because there are those who desire to roll back our achievements.

These changes have been initiated on both sides of aisles of Congress. Creating ID laws, altering the Civil Rights Act, closing voting sites, and gerrymandering are some of the ways of creating an unequal political playing field that could shift the balance of power for decades in the favor of one party.[32] Malcolm X said, "We, the Black masses, don't want these leaders who seek our support coming to us representing a certain political party. They must come to us today as Black Leaders representing the welfare of Black people. We won't follow any leader today who comes on the basis of political party."[33]

Both parties (Democrats and Republicans) are controlled by the same people who have abused our rights, and who have deceived us with false promises every time an election rolls around. The ability to navigate through the two-party system can be quite interesting concerning their diverse path. The current Republicans claim to be the party of Lincoln; however, the Republican Party was started to confront the atrocities of slavery legislated by the Democrats. The Democrats were staunchly for slavery and did everything in their power to maintain this oppressive system of living for Blacks.

Fast forward to today you will find the same type of debauchery; they are overtly telling you what to expect, how to expect the change, and when to expect the change. In fact, instead of investing money in education and job creation programs, billions of dollars was directed into building prisons that house an extraordinary number of blacks.[34]

The political clout that blacks currently hold has been negated because of being made to believe our issues are not in line with mainstream America. We have been made to believe they cannot think for ourselves so someone else has to perform this task. We do not need other people to think for us, we need the space to make up our own minds and plot our own course.

We should no longer settle for the "I know what is best for you" mentality. We should open their eyes to the reality of being used by both parties for the advancement of our own agenda, to not be blinded by the opportunity of selling their vote to the highest bidder in order to "move up" the ladder of success. Malcolm X said "You're not supposed to be so blind with patriotism that you can't face reality. Wrong is wrong, no matter who says it."[35]

There is a yearning for freedom and being engaged in the political process is one way to ensure your concerns are voiced and logged. The time is coming for blacks to stop being dependent upon the two-party system and rise up to create a black nationalist movement similar to the idea of Marcus Garvey. It is time for black people in America to have a defined agenda, a well thought out plan for addressing these issues, and a model for community engagement.

We have to learn how to protest with a reason. We have to understand how the political system does not favor the loud and disruptive, but the persistent. We have to continue the good fight and be politically resolute because Mahatma Ghandi said, "To deprive a man of his natural liberty and to deny to him the ordinary amenities of life is worse than starving the body; it is starvation of the soul, the dweller in the body."[36] Blacks have been devoid of this right for over 400 years, but have just begun to realize the rise of potential of power exerted through being accepted as full citizens.

Blacks have to build the courage to denounce the senselessness around them and rise to higher heights in the pursuit of social, economic, and political justice. We have to learn not to fight one another in order to accomplishment these goals. It is a given that everyone will not agree with everyone one hundred percent of the time; however, we cannot fight and tear down one another in the name of progress. I think Malcolm X illustrated this thought the best when he said, "We black men have a hard enough time in our own struggle for justice, and already have enough enemies as it is, to make the drastic mistake of attacking each other and adding more weight to an already unbearable load."[37]

The question on the minds of many blacks is what now? What more needs to be done in order to be accepted? How do we flex our political muscle? Dr. King said "I refuse to accept the view that mankind is so tragically bound to the starless midnight of racism and war that the bright daybreak of peace and brotherhood can never become a reality. I believe that unarmed truth and unconditional love will have the final word."[38] The future of blacks in America is bright, but the ominous words of Dr. King still rings true that we are in a starless night of racism.

The political system in America is broken beyond repair and it is requiring a new set of people with colorblind objectives to populate it. We have been seeing our political views through various colored glasses. We need politicians who are not afraid to stand up for the rights of all the people, not just the ones who can afford to attend expensive dinners or can pay to play. The politics of this country is shifting and we must be ever on guard lest we fall into the slumber of mediocracy and sleepwalk around the issues. We must stand our ground and be vocal about our beliefs.

Recently, a number of sports figures started protesting the national anthem by refusing to stand. Many Americans are upset by this and sought to call those who were taking a stand as being unpatriotic. Mike Ditka when asked about Colin Kaepernick's political stance said, "I think it's a problem...anybody who disrespects this country and the flag." Ditka further stated, "If they don't like the country they don't like our flag. …get the hell out."[39]

Another op-ed writer, Dr. Jim Ferguson, in the Knoxville Focus, spoke his mind about the players, their money, and the NFLs allowing the protest to take place. He said in his weekly column that he is "sick and tired of the opinions of activist jocks..."[40] I think both he and Ditka need to understand these "jock activists" have been around for decades. Ask Muhammed Ali, Tommie Smith, John Carlos, Arthur Ashe, Jackie Robinson, Jesse Owens, Satchel Page, and all the other black athletes that were shunned because of their skin color and the fight they had to prove their relevance.

These "jocks" made it their point to let the world know that the sports world is not oblivious to what is happening in society because they have to function in that broken system. Blacks, especially black athletes, should now recognize the forum in which they live. They are told to be "good blacks" and make other people money, but you better not stir the pot by caring about the others in your community by being politically savvy.

Since the time of his column, the country has selected Donald J. Trump to be the 45th President of the United States. He famously asked the blacks in this country what do you have to lose in regards to education, employment, and economics. Many have railed against this and his campaign, but how many people have taken the time to internalized and reflect on this statement? This could be the beginning to create an agenda of action against blacks and other minorities.

This is why blacks need to have local and national agendas in which we can ban together for the good of the whole population. We need to stop posturing and protest for real change with our time and our money. Until this occurs, we will continue to be bought and sold by the highest bidder every two to four years.

The problems of Black America have been the same prior to the election of Donald Trump and they have been the same for the past 40 years, except the problem is becoming greater with the passing of each subsequent generation. The time for self-reflection and self-motivation is over, now is the time has commenced for the creation of an agenda to ensure our dreams and opportunities are not railroaded. Time can either be our best friend or worst enemy depending on how we respond. I hope we choose wisely.

EDUCATION

Long ago, people traveled from the far corners of the earth to study in Africa. It was the continent that created mathematics, built the majestic pyramids, and openly bestowed its wisdom to all who passed through its doors. The culture, wealth, and knowledge of Africa was plundered by explorers, who stripped the country of its wealth and slaughtered its people in return as a gift for their hospitality.

I wondered aloud about the use of hieroglyphics and where they can be found. There are only three places in the known world to have used such markings; Egypt, Mayans, and Southeast Asia. This means the world received education from the Africans, and maybe it would be a stretch of the imagination to think the Africans traveled to these countries and taught them, as well as learning about their culture in return. Now, the world has whited out the accomplishments of blacks, none more like in the United States.

A poignant phrase says the writing of history always favors those who were on the winning side. However, we have generations of children not knowing and understanding the important role blacks played in the creation, maintenance, and advancement of this country. Most will have never heard of many of this inventors who used their minds to create items that are used in our everyday life

Even though blacks were limited by traditional educational standards, they were trailblazers for the science and technology we use today. The innovative genius of Lewis

Latimer (carbon filament), Garrett Morgan (stop

light/gas mask), Jan Matzeliger (shoe lasting

machine), George Crum (potato chip), Miriam

Benjamin (gong and signal chair), Daniel Hale

Williams (open heart surgery), Marie Van

Brittan Brown (home security system), Madame

C.J. Walker (hair care product empire), and

Lloyd Hall (food preservation) are remembered

today as we utilize their inventions in our

everyday lives.

Today, we still have brilliant minds

achieving in the fields of math, science, and

technology. However, blacks are still not

achieving the educational goals necessary to

compete with the growing needs of society.

Blacks have always cherished education because

they understood its effects. Malcolm X stated that education is the passport of the future, so based on our current educational statistics, our future might be bleak unless we begin to motivate our school-aged children to be the best they can be in all areas of their development.

However, our children are statistically becoming a reflection of what we value. According to the National Center for Education Statistics (NCES), the public school graduation rate for blacks is 70.7%, which is more than 10% below the national rate of 81.4%[41], which means almost 30% of our students are not completing high school. NCES also reported that 7.9% of blacks drop out of school, which represents 315,000 students.[42]

In review of college acceptance rates at four year institutions, 34.9% of blacks were accepted, which is below the national average of 40.5%, yet 21.4% of black students starting in 2008 finished within four years.[43] The graduation rates for black students after six years is 40.9% versus the national average 59.6%.[44] So in comparison, the data shows blacks are below the average of getting accepted into college and once there take more than four years to graduation, which means they are in jeopardy of not completing their post-secondary education.[45]

Despite all the recent advances in our educational journey, we are still not reaching the heights of educational success as seen in other racial groups. Our lag is due to those who think we still do not have a place around the table of education and success even though there are cries for equality and diversity in the academic community. We do not have black teachers in the classroom; if fact, 17% of teachers in this country are minorities, so we are still seeing a disparity where it matters most.[46]

Another point of interest is the push for school vouchers, where public tax dollars will be used to fund private education. Those pushing for this system highlight how they will benefit children by not having them attend failing schools, have better curriculums, and have better structure. Those in opposition cite the need for community schools, using tax dollars to benefit everyone and not a select few, and the quest to privatize the educational system in the United States. In hearing all the arguments for and against the system, most have forgotten the history behind why this private school phenomena first came to light and why we should be guarded with its sudden resurgence and popularity.

America has long been a denier of rights to blacks, a practice that goes back to the inception of this country. So severe were these practices that laws were actually enacted that prohibited slaves from learning to read and write, but thought it good to have a few that could read.[47] The black slave was only three-fifths of a person, was considered property, and sometimes the occasional pet. However, this did not quench their desire to learn and become educated so they too could enjoy "life, liberty, and the pursuit of happiness."

Brown versus the Board of Education of Topeka changed the landscape of education in this country. It removed one of the final hurdles surrounding blacks following the Civil War. Many of the Jim Crow laws were enacted to maintain the separate but equal doctrine and to maintain the superiority complex of the races. These laws were created to circumvent these rights through creating loophole laws despite the passage of the Civil War Amendments that abolished slavery, granted voting rights to blacks, and guaranteed citizenship to blacks.

The passage of those laws saw a burst in the rise of black schools to educate the former slaves and their children. Brown v. Board of Education of Topeka opened the door to discuss educational segregation and Chief Justice Earl

Warren proceeded to take the door off its hinges. Warren, who heard the argument for desegregation from Thurgood Marshall, said in the unanimous opinion "that in the field of public education the doctrine of 'separate but equal' has no place. Separate educational facilities are inherently unequal."[48]

After this decision, the birth of private schools grew in America because whites refused to have their children in the same classroom as blacks. As a result, some jurisdictions diverted public money to fund the private schools, which resulted in the public schools attended by the black students were underfunded.[49]

So what lessons have been learned from this history? Today, we are seeing a rise of charter schools that will be funded with public funds, and we have legislators pushing for vouchers to let taxpayer money fund private education to the detriment of local school districts. Sound familiar? This was the same rhetoric and attitude held by the ruling party during a dark time in our history, and we are doomed to repeat it unless we fully understand the ramifications of these impending bills.

This flight from public education, coupled with their economic plan, should have people paying attention to what it occurring, the death of public education as we know it. The fight for equal education and recognition is as old as the United States, but education in the 21st century and beyond is another issue for blacks. What will our collective response be to this situation?

We must fight back to avoid another 'separate but equal' paradigm occur in this country.

A CALL TO ACTION

Donald Trump famously said, "You're living in poverty, your schools are no good, you have no jobs, 58% of your youth is unemployed -- what the hell do you have to lose?"[50] Sometimes a message can be rejected because of the messenger. In this instance, Trump was talking to an all white audience in Michigan about the problems of Black America

From a political standpoint, he is appealing for votes. From a common sense standpoint, he is on the money. With complete skepticism, let us intellectually separate the message from the messenger. What if Dr. Martin Luther King, Jr., Malcolm X, Denzel Washington, or Oprah Winfrey espoused a similar sentiment? I would probably think this message would have been fully embraced and the media would have labeled it as a clarion bell for improvement.

I would call for saner heads to prevail and really take stock into these words, not because they came from Donald Trump, but because sometimes the truth hurts and one does not want to face the reality of their living, especially when it comes from someone deemed to be an "outsider." I followed this election with earnest intellect because I desired to comprehend the platforms of the candidates and how they would truly bridge the racial gap that resonates like an echo in the Grand Canyon. After the election, I cautiously tuned my ears to hear how the country would rebound from a bitter election. Sometimes desires are not fulfilled; however, the revelation about hope and change would not die, it is simply transforming in a way where one must be prepared to accept the change or be willing to aggressively advocate for another direction to benefit society.

The ability to aggressively advocate or my favorite term, protest with a purpose, has been a staple of American democracy. The quote by Trump should be a frightening alarm rather than a soft wakeup call because it is a generation of children that hang in its delicate balance. Black Americans took this as a racial insult and the Democratic Party considered this as Trump being out of touch and racially bigoted.

The media portrayed him as a white man who will never be able to overcome a white-dominated philosophy. However, there was a small minority of people that embraced the words as a challenge to change stagnated thoughts and actions. I fall within the last line of these thoughts because I do believe it is an opportunity to not provide another political party the chance to use blacks as political pawns.

Malcolm X said, "I for one believe that if you give people a thorough understanding of what confronts them and the basic causes that produce it, they'll create their own program, and when the people create a program, you get action."[51] The past generations of blacks in America realized the problem of their day and sought for a way to burst through the walls of ignorance and hate. The end result was the creation of programs that both benefited and harmed blacks in this country. However, I will say some progress is better than none, but now the burden has shifted to the present day state of the black community, which should be both concerning and alarming because blacks have (1) lost their sense of community, (2) forgotten their place in the annals of history, and (3) deferred their spiritual authority to the whims of societal opinions.

Black America cannot ask other people to do what they have refused to do for themselves. There cannot be an expectation of 'us' without the inclusion of 'we'. The generation of thinkers have been replaced by a generation of expecters. This shift has heightened the lack of protesting with a purpose because we do not understand the issues being placed before us.

The movement for change cannot move the consciousness of society because it cannot logically define its purpose. Therefore the lack of purpose causes the message to get dismissed as propaganda, so it will take delivering a powerful statement with people dedicated to making a difference. The civil rights activists of the 60s staged sit-ins, stand-ins, and marches to actively petition change in the face of adversity.

Blacks have forgotten their roots and it gets dimmer with each subsequent generation. They have taken their place in society for granted; they have forgotten how the precious rights they possess were forged in blood, sweat, and tears. These rights are now being taken away with the swipe of a pen.

This is transpiring because the lack of understanding cultural identity and consciousness is eroding. Blacks have forgotten their royal heritage, educational accomplishments, and societal fights to become entertainers and performers. The study of poetry, literature, and the arts has been replaced with sports, music, and other forms of empty entertainment.

Black America represents a one trillion dollar economic block, but have we demanded an equal opportunity to profit from these ventures? We complain about the system, yet we relish in profiteering and scamming the system. We are comfortable with sustaining the system of generational poverty that was established to stunt our growth and hinder our progress. We are comfortable with having several children for the "checks and stamps". In other words, we are birthing children we cannot possibly afford or sustain without government assistance.

Blacks who lived during the civil rights era can remember a time when blacks would not accept any type of assistance from the government because it was seen as an extension of the segregation, hate, and racial apathy during their time. Today, this sense of pride has turned into a big hand out with the establishment of entitlements, which was probably one of the worst decisions ever enacted by the government. The black family structure has crumbled and has become weak and ineffective because it no longer has a strong family core. The lack of family structure has weakened the community, which in turns weakens the activities and program of the community, and has allowed the criminal element to gain a powerful footprint in the community.

Blacks live the wrong dream by peddling drugs, committing crimes, and recruiting the young minds of the community into gangs. The children, whose family structure is lacking or non-existent, are being drawn into this life because they are seeking love and attention. Schools become battlegrounds because seeking education is attuned to not being black, so being smart becomes a disease within the community, which is shocking considering the previous generations regarded education as the passport to success. However, the school system celebrates failure, yet they are pushing to privatize the educational system, a venture similar to the reaction of the community when

Brown v. Board of Education of Topeka was successfully adjudicated in 1950 to integrate school systems across the nation.

History is bound to repeat itself when it is not learned, internalized, and passed on. Let's reflect back to the slavery days when this country was fighting over the institution of slavery. Don't let anyone think this was about state's rights or the abridgement of the federal government, it was solely about whether the institution of slavery would be the norm in the United States.

Alexander Stephens, Vice President of the Confederate States of America, in 1861 said, "The Confederacy, by contrast, is founded upon exactly the opposite idea; its foundations are laid, its cornerstone rests, upon the great truth

100

that the Negro is not equal to the white man; that slavery, subordination to the superior race is his natural and moral condition."[52] This war might be over, but blacks are still fighting a civil war, a grand battle for cultural and intellectual control.

The black community cannot wait for a savior. President Obama was not the promised savior the black community desired him to be because he represented the entire country. This led to disappointment because our hands were out waiting to be filled instead of reaching out to grasp opportunities.

The black community should not have expected President Obama to resuscitate a community's problem that has existed for decades. True to its saying, most people do not appreciate or realize what they have until it is gone; however, the black community cannot wait for things to be taken away before answering the bell. To use a boxing term, we have been knocked down and given a standing eight count. Afterwards, if more punishment is absorbed without fighting back, the referee will declare the fight over as a technical knockout.

The subsequent years for blacks cannot be called the year of the knockout, it cannot be the decade of futility, and it cannot be the century of rollbacks. This is the time for change, and those who will answer the call to be the change agents must be ready to accept the challenge and dare to stand up for what is right. Only then can the road to progress begin to benefit all the citizens of this country.

So maybe Donald Trump has a point about challenging the black community to think more about its past, present, and future. Black America should not be outraged by the message, they should be outraged by the message of self-destruction being announced to the world. The black community should be outraged they have underperforming schools, drug problems, black on black crime, children that cannot excel academically, and generational welfare. The black community should be adamant about demanding more of itself, circle the wagons, acknowledge the problem, create programs, and work to have the program be successfully accomplished.

Black America has been blinded by misguided success, bamboozled, hoodwinked, and lead astray. We have been falsely lead to believe we have been truly integrated into the fabric of this society; however, we have been sold a false bill of rights. It is time for a new message to be broadcast because the black community cannot afford to have over 60 years of progress be rescinded by bad choices and political overtures.

There is a stated vision for America to return to the life of the 1950s, the good old days of the Cleavers. Those were the good old days for one segment of the population and a nightmare for all the others. If Black America's desire is to move from here to there and not have the hands of time be reversed, we need to be more vocal and stand up for justice and equality.

If we do nothing and allow this false vision to become reality, we will be living in the land of 50s television, once again on the outside looking in, wondering when will change occur. If we do nothing, we will have more than a lost generation on our hands; we will have a lost people wandering in the darkness, not sure of when we will ever see the light.

AFTERWORD

I hope this book has encouraged you to not stay where you are, but to move onward and upward toward bigger and better things. We cannot be satisfied with the status quo in this time of local, national, and global unrest. Black America must be willing to return to a time when we believed in family and community. This concept of community was strong during the civil rights struggle, but we have seemed to have forgotten those days because those stories of sacrifice have been transformed into myths and folk tales.

Knowledge is power and we are becoming weak because we are not tapping into this unlimited power source. We are falling prey to the trap established to keep us from rising to the top. We are being kept down because we are distracted by the noise that prevents us from focusing on what is truly important. We are distracted from bettering ourselves so we can strengthen our community.

We can only be ourselves, but we do not have to be tied to the stake of stubbornness, the harness of hate, the pole of poor outcomes, and hold the reins of ruin. We must understand this is a country where not everyone agrees with the individual right to life and liberty. We live in a country where being different is not accepted. We live in a country where not accepting the status quo can have grave consequences.

America has not learned the lessons of 18th century indifference, 19th century slavery, and 20th century oppression. We have carried these stigmas and beliefs into the 21st century and we are surely doomed to repeat the mistakes of the past if we continue down this path. There is a scripture in the bible that asks if we are our brother's keeper and the answer is absolutely, irrefutably, and unapologetically yes!

I believe the ability to have a sense of community and truly care for people in the community is the first step of reclamation. The second step of reclamation is acknowledging the present condition of the community and find ways to change the future. The third step of reclamation is action. The black community cannot be satisfied with meeting for the sake of meeting and not move towards placing those plans and ideas into action. This plan cannot progress through degradation, shouting, and not making logical points; we must transcend this conversation to levels where we can truly enact change.

This level of change starts at home and the change agents are parents, families, and community members who are not afraid to stand up and be accountable for their role in either building or destroying the community. We can have all the movements we desire, but the movement of action can only be accomplished by getting in front of our elected officials and make them feel our concerns. If not, we must start producing viable candidates who have the whole community in mind and not just the ones with money.

We must reclaim our people from the lake of despair. We must return to the day when someone said "I'm black and I'm proud" that those words could truly be felt and believed. We have to return to being a helping hand instead of a chopping hand. We must regain our belief in our intellect, craftsmanship, and entrepreneurial spirit.

We have to support each other and build bridges instead of tearing each other down. We have to stop buying into society's stereotype and create new ways of thinking and exploring. We have to rise to the top lest we sink in the quicksand of distractions.

These are the choices we have to make if we truly want to get to a place where we have the true freedom we seek. How do we reach this destination?

There is only one way…Together!!!

BIBLIOGRAPHY

[1] Alexander, Amy. (1998). *The Farrakhan Factor*. Grove Press: New York, NY

[2] Clegg II, Legrand. (1997). Ebonics: A Serious Analysis of African American Speech Patterns.
http://www.melanet.com/clegg_series/ebonic s.html

[3] IBID.

[4] IBID.

[5] Schiavo, Renata. (2007). *Health Communication: From Theory to Practice*. San Francisco, Josey-Bass.

[6] Statistic Brain Research Institute (2014). African American Black Statistics.

[7] Kalahar, Dean. The Decline of the African American Family. American Thinker, March 29, 2014.
http://www.americanthinker.com/articles/201 4/03/the_decline_of_the_africanamerican_fa mily.html

[8] IBID.

[9] National Healthy Marriage Resource Center. African Americans and Black Community.
http://www.healthymarriageinfo.org/research -and-policy/marriage-facts/culture/african-americans-and-black-community/index.aspx

[10] Hymowitz, Kay. (2005). The Black Family: 40 Years of Lies. City Journal, August 25, 2005.   http://www.city-journal.org/html/black-family-40-years-lies-

12872.html

[11] IBID.

[12] Discoverthenetworks.org. Breakdown of the Black Family, and Its Consequences, February 14, 2005. http://www.discoverthenetworks.org/viewSubCategory.asp?id=1261

[13] Blankenhorn, David. (1995). *Fatherless America*. New York, NY: BasicBooks.

[14] IBID.

[15] IBID.

[16] Steinberg, Laurence. (2004). The 10 Basic Principles of Good Parenting. New York, NY: Simon & Schuster

[17] Religious Landscape Study. Pew Research Center, Washington, DC (June 4, 2014). http://www.pewforum.org/religious-landscape-study/racial-and-ethnic-composition

[18] IBID.

[19] Sewell, Said. (2001). African American Religion: The Struggle for Community Development in a Southern City. *Journal of Southern Religion.*

[20] Washington, Joseph. *Christian Century*, May 1, 1974, p. 472-475. http://religion-online.org/showarticle.asp?title=1610

[21] IBID.

[22] Savage, Barbara. The Myth of the Black Church. Religion and Politics, June 7, 2012. http://religionandpolitics.org/2012/06/07/the-myth-of-the-black-church

[23] Mellowes, Marilyn. The Black Church. PBS:

Frontline, God in America (October 11, 2010). http://www.pbs.org/godinamerica/black-church/

[24] Cooley, Charles H. (1902). Human Nature and the Social Order. New York: Scribner's.

[25] Robbins, Anthony. & McClendon III, Joseph. (1997). Unlimited Power: A Black Choice. New York, NY: Fireside

[26] Sowell, Thomas. Blacks Suffer Lasting Damage From 'Favors.' Knoxville News Sentinel, September 29, 2016.

[27] Lerner, Michael. & West, Cornell. (1995). Jews & Blacks: Let the Healing Begin. New York, NY: Grosset/Putnam.

[28] Barton, David. (2003). The History of Black Voting Rights. http://www.freerepublic.com/focus/f-news/1072053/posts

[29] Black Leaders During Reconstruction. http://www.history.com/topics/american-civil-war/black-leaders-during-reconstruction

[30] Statistic Brain. (2016). African American Black Statistics. http://www.statisticbrain.com/african-american-black-statistics/

[31] Arnwine, Barbara & Johnson-Blanco, M. (2013). Voting Rights at a Crossroads. Economic Policy Institute. http://www.epi.org/publication/voting-rights-crossroads-supreme-court-decision/

[32] Shelby County v. Holder 570 U.S.__ (2013).

[33] Malcolm X. http://www.malcolm-

x.org/quotes.htm

[34] Alexander, Michelle. (2016). The Clinton Legacy is Black Impoverishment-So Why Are We Still Voting for Hillary? The Root. http://www.theroot.com/articles/politics/2016/02/the_clinton_legacy_decimated_black_america_so_why_are_we_still_voting_for/3/

[35] Malcolm X.
http://www.brainyquote.com/quotes/authors/m/malcolm_x.html

[36] Mahatma Ghandi.
http://www.brainyquote.com/quotes/authors/m/mahatma_gandhi_4.html

[37] Malcolm X. http://www.malcolm-x.org/quotes.htm

[38] Rev. Dr. Martin Luther King, Jr. http://www.brainyquote.com/quotes/authors/m/martin_luther_king_jr.html

[39] Augustine, Bernie. (2016). Mike Ditka Has 'No Respect for Colin Kaepernick,' Says He Doesn't See The 'Atrocities' NFL Players Are Protesting. New York Daily News, September 23, 2016.

[40] Ferguson, Jim. (2016). I've had it! Knoxville Focus. September 26, 2016.

[41] National Center for Education Statistics (2015). ED*Facts*/Consolidated State Performance Report, SY 2012–13, http://www2.ed.gov/admins/lead/account/consolidated/index.html.

[42] IBID.

[43] IBID.

[44] IBID.

[45] African American Black Statistics – Statistic Brain (2016). 2017 Statistic Brain Research Institute, publishing as Statistic Brain. http://www.statisticbrain.com/african-american-black-statistics/

[46] Deruy, Emily. Student Diversity Is Up But Teachers Are Mostly White. https://aacte.org/news-room/aacte-in-the-news/347-student-diversity-is-up-but-teachers-are-mostly-white

[47] Haskins, Jim. (1998). *The Dream and the Struggle: Separate But Not Equal.* Scholastic, Inc.: New York, NY

[48] IBID.

[49] IBID.

[50] Lebianco, Tom & Killough, Ashley. (2016). Trump Pitches Black Voters: 'What the Hell Do You Have to Lose?' Http://www.cnn.com/2016/08/18/politics/donaldtrump-african-american-voters/index.html

[51] Goodreads. http://www.goodreads.com/quotes/797-i-for-one-believe-that-if-you-give-people-a

[52] Blake, John & Sambou, Tawanda. (2016). How Trump's Victory Turns Into Another 'Lost Cause.' http://www.cnn.com/2016/12/28/us/lost-cause-trump/